For Nicholas (who likes coffee) and Oskar (who likes milk).
We make the best team. — D.W.

For Marika, Suraya, Paulina, Nat, Scott,
and the rest of the tea family. — C.O.

# TEATIME
## around the world

**DENYSE WAISSBLUTH**                    **CHELSEA O'BYRNE**

GREYSTONE KIDS
GREYSTONE BOOKS • VANCOUVER/BERKELEY/LONDON

Tea for one.

Tea for two.

Tea for me.

Tea for you.

With sugar

Green tea, mint, and sugar are mixed to make sweet
Moroccan mint tea. Guests are served three cups—
each has a slightly different taste.

or spice,

On almost every street corner in India, masala chai is sold by vendors called chai wallahs. Strong tea and spices like cinnamon, ginger, cloves, cardamom, and pepper are boiled with milk and sweetened.

# yak butter

Po cha, or butter tea, is traditional in Tibet. A brick of dark tea is simmered in water. Later, milk, yak-milk butter, and salt are added. The mixture is churned until it's thick like creamy soup, then sipped from a wooden bowl.

or ice.

Thai iced tea, or cha yen, is popular with locals and tourists in Thailand. Strongly brewed sweet tea is poured over ice and drunk from a bag through a straw. Street vendors sell it from their carts.

# With berries

Indigenous cultures in North America prepare tea from berries, plants, and roots. These can be used to treat fevers, colds, and sore backs, or even to help people sleep.

# or flowers,

While the hibiscus plant is originally from West Africa,
it has inspired tisanes around the world. In South Sudan, karkadé,
or hibiscus tea, is made with hibiscus petals. It tastes tart
like cranberries and is served hot or iced and sometimes sweetened.

enjoy it for hours.

Matcha, or powdered green tea, is carefully prepared and served during chanoyu, the Japanese tea ceremony. Each part of the ritual helps to create a harmonious atmosphere and make sure guests enjoy the experience.

# With sweet things

In Russia, guests are served a strong black tea called zavarka, which is brewed in a special pot, the samovar. They can add extra hot water, milk, sugar, or jam to taste. And it would be rude not to offer guests a snack, like cake or cookies.

# stacked high,

After an English duchess once complained of being hungry between lunch and dinner, the tradition of afternoon tea was started. Now enjoyed worldwide, this custom involves serving trays of goodies like finger sandwiches; scones with butter, jam, and cream; and cakes. And, of course, tea.

or poured from the sky.

Teh tarik, or "pulled tea," is the national drink of Malaysia and is made with strong black tea and condensed milk. It's poured from up high, or "pulled" between two mugs, to make it frothy. Preparing this tea can be quite a show!

With soda,

In Pakistan, a luxurious pink chai is made with pistachios, almonds, salt, milk, and spices. Baking soda is added, which enhances the flavor and pink color.

# a rock,

In Iran, the samovar bubbles from morning prayers until the sun sets so that the reddish-brown tea can be enjoyed all day. It Is usually served on a silver tray with a bright yellow rock candy called nabat.

# or made with a sock.

In Hong Kong, a popular drink is made by slowly straining tea and milk
through a special filter that looks like a sock. Because of the sock-like filter,
it is often called silk stocking tea.

# From old ways

Tea, known as cha in China, was first discovered thousands of years ago and is still an important part of life. A traditional preparation for the gongfu tea ceremony involves several steps and special utensils. Guests sit around a host, who serves multiple infusions of the tea in a small teapot. Tea pets, which are miniature figurines, are used for good luck.

to new,

Bubble tea was created in the 1980s in Taiwan. This tasty drink is made with different kinds of tea with powdered milk and syrup. What makes it extra special are the tapioca balls mixed in, which are like chewy bubbles and give the tea its name.

# with straws to drink through.

Mate is popular in countries like Argentina, Chile, and Uruguay. Like true tea, mate is made from leaves steeped in hot water, but they are from the yerba mate plant. Served in a hollow gourd, it is drunk through a special straw called a bombilla.

Good friends will appear
when teatime is here.

In the Caribbean, roselle hibiscus buds are harvested from early fall to winter. In Jamaica, the festive drink is known as sorrel. Deep crimson in color, it is often spiced with ginger, cloves, and sugar.

Tea for one.
Tea for two.

Loved by all
the whole world through.

# My Tea Story

We call a lot of different drinks "tea." "True" tea is made from the *Camellia sinensis* plant. Herbal teas, or tisanes, are still considered teas, but made from other plants, berries, herbs, or flowers. Whatever the ingredients, teas are always steeped in boiling water to bring out their aroma and flavor.

While there are different stories about the world's first cup of tea, the drink, which originated in China, is thousands of years old. Throughout the centuries, it has grown in popularity, traveling to all corners of the globe, where it has been adapted to reflect local customs and traditions.

While the history, evolution, and even the name for tea differ around the world, for me, tea has been a natural way to connect with people and learn about new cultures. My earliest memories of tea stem from my grandparents' farm in the Canadian Prairies, where a kettle of strong black tea was always on, ready to greet guests. As I started to travel, tea remained a symbol of hospitality.

Once, while in Singapore during Ramadan, I visited a local night market. I stood in awe as a man entertained crowds by quickly pouring a frothy, steaming drink between two cups. One family, who saw my interest in the custom, invited me to join them for a drink of the mysterious beverage as they broke their fast. And that's how I was introduced to a local tea, teh tarik. We drank, ate, and talked for hours, sharing ideas about our respective countries, backgrounds, and cultures.

While my experience with tea is based on warmth and hospitality, like all stories, different people have different perspectives. While this book is not able or intended to cover the full history and evolution of the drink, or all of the people who have helped shape it, I hope it gives you a little taste of tea's magic. May all your days be "steeped" in wonder and surrounded by friends!

— D.W.

A special thanks to Aisha Kiani, founder of I Dream Library; Sebastian Beckwith, founder of In Pursuit of Tea; Shabnam Weber from the Tea and Herbal Association of Canada; Maiko Behr of SaBi Tea Arts; "teaexpert" Adam Scott; Yoko Riley, Senior Instructor Emerita—Japanese, University of Calgary; Julie Flett; and Anastasia Martin-Stilwell, Indigenous Lead, Travel Alberta, with the support of Indigenous Tourism Alberta, for their valuable contributions in reviewing the book.

We invite you to be curious and join us on this special and delicious journey around the world. — Denyse & Chelsea

Text copyright © 2020 by Denyse Waissbluth
Illustrations copyright © 2020 by Chelsea O'Byrne

23 24 25 26 27  8 7 6 5 4

All rights reserved. No part of this book may be reproduced, stored in a retrieval system or transmitted, in any form or by any means, without the prior written consent of the publisher or a license from The Canadian Copyright Licensing Agency (Access Copyright). For a copyright license, visit accesscopyright.ca or call toll free to 1-800-893-5777.

Greystone Kids / Greystone Books Ltd.
greystonebooks.com

Cataloguing data available from Library and Archives Canada
978-1-77164-601-7 (cloth)
978-1-77164-602-4 (epub)

Editing by Kallie George
Copy editing by Antonia Banyard
Proofreading by DoEun Kwon
Jacket and interior design by Sara Gillingham Studio
Jacket illustration by Chelsea O'Byrne

Printed and bound in China on FSC® certified paper at Shenzhen Reliance Printing.
The FSC® label means that materials used for the product have been responsibly sourced.

Greystone Books thanks the Canada Council for the Arts, the British Columbia Arts Council, the Province of British Columbia through the Book Publishing Tax Credit, and the Government of Canada for supporting our publishing activities.

Greystone Books gratefully acknowledges the xʷməθkʷəy̓əm (Musqueam), Sḵwx̱wú7mesh (Squamish), and səlilwətaɬ (Tsleil-Waututh) peoples on whose land our Vancouver head office is located.